Love Letters from the Lieutenant

Jim Carland
with his partner through time, JoAnn

This is a work of love. Its sole purpose is to tell the love story between two unknown lovers whose time together on this plane was far too short, but whose time together on the next plane shall know no end.

They both believe that theirs is the greatest love story ever told.

You, Dear Reader, shall be the judge!

Copyright © 2013 by Whitney Press, Inc.

Novels by JoAnn and Jim Carland

Featuring Tori and Jace:
Prometheus Unleashed
A Killing in the Market
Flight of the Phoenix

Featuring the Carson Family:
Hidden Malice
The Case of the Junk Yard Dog
Reaping the Whirlwind

ISBN: 978-1-932155-63-1

Published in the U.S. by Whitney Press, Arden, North Carolina

Lieutenant James and Mrs. JoAnn Carland
June 12, 1971

Contents

Introduction 1
My Greatest Joy 3
First Love: Last Love 5
Joy! 9
Home! 11
The Wind 13
Firelight 15
Snowflakes! 17
With Child! 19
Each Morn 21
Making Out 23
Growing Older 25
Drawing Eyes 27
Mother's Love 29
Sweetheart! 31
Your Glance 33
Working Together 37
Together 39
Your Embrace 41
Laughter! 43
True Love 45
Making Love 47
Teddy Bears 49
Passion 51
Summer's Eve 53
Awake! 55
Gentle 57
Why Thee I Love 59

A Taste of Salt	63
Catching Eyes	65
My Pain	67
Kisses	71
Her Mind	73
Mornings!	75
Fishing	77
Answer, God!	79
Smiles	81
Cherry Pink	83
Blest and Curst!	85
First Kiss, Last Kiss	87
The Last Ballad	91
I Have No Gift for Thee	95
Twenty	99
Thirty Years of Christmas My Love Hath Given Me	101
With this Ring	103
My Wife	105
Sweetheart	107
Catching the Dream	111
Jo Ann	113
Ode to Stella Grace	117
List to Me!	121
Sun Rise, Sun Set	123
To a Fellow Lover	125
Butterflies	127
I love you	129

Dedication

To all those who Love!

My fondest wish is that you, Dear Reader, will find words in this little tome that will touch your heart, and make the love that you feel for your own love a little more tender, a little sweeter, a little stronger.

Please share these words with your love.

I wish you love, Dear Reader, a love as strong as mine!

Introduction

My Angel, My Muse, My Sweetheart, My Love, awakened from this dream of life on August 15, 2013, and left me yet dreaming. To say that I was devastated is not to understand in the slightest the pain I felt. I lost my heart, I lost my mind, I lost my will to live.

My Darling spoke to me on September 2, as I was preparing her Celebration, and told me to write this book. She speaks to me yet, and most of the words in this book, that appear after she awoke, I truly believe came from her.

This, I say to you, Dear Reader, let not a day go by without speaking your love. Go speak it now! Your lover needs hear thee!

I met My Love when we were but six years of age, in the first year of school. When we were eighteen, I proposed, fearing the separation that college was about to create. My Love demurred. She said, quite rightly, that I was confused and distressed. She loved me, she swore, and I believed her. She just did not think a marriage between us would work until I exorcized the demons that plagued me. How right she was! The tale is clear in the letters that I wrote to her in the years that followed. We wrote each other from 1965 until 1971. I rushed through college with overloads and into the Marine Corps, for the war was raging and I wanted to be there, to risk my life, to taste the fear, to experience it all! It was a soldier of fortune I wanted to be!

You can see from that, Dear Reader, that I did, indeed, have demons. The war did what My Love wanted. It made me grow up. When I returned, I was a man, and she came to me!

She came to me!

My Greatest Joy

The joy thou dost give me, My Love, tis vast!
Tis more than I can hold, My Heart, tis huge!
I ween that joy, My Love, dost all surpass!
My heart doth burst, My Love, with love for you!

Thy kiss, so sweet, so soft, such joy, such bliss!
Thee builds our love, our kiss, upon this pyre!
And still, my world doth shake, from this, your kiss!
Your touch inflames! I can't contain this fire!

To hold thee close, make love to thee, divine!
The fire, the flame, love so vast tis Heaven!
Thou clasps me tight, to thy sweet breast, sublime!
No end to this, hearts afire doth beckon!

But greater still is this! My hand, thou takes!
To hold your hand, just that, my world doth make!

I wrote this on June 12, 1997. It was our 26st anniversary. Today, it speaks to me in a way that makes my world stop spinning. It was, and is, the single greatest piece I have ever written.

First Love: Last Love

That First Love is so very special; our minds return to those days again and again as time drives our lives; we remember the kisses, the soft sighs, the glances, the promises made and shared.

They are sweet, these memories; they can make us smile; they can make us weep; and though our eyes grow dim, the face of First Love shines ever bright in our hearts.

You were my First Love.

I remember our first kiss; I thought the world moved; I remember, My Love, I remember it all.

Last Love; the one that endures; it is the Last Love that carries us through life; that grows stronger, day by day; that gives us courage to withstand hardship; that quietly supports us as we struggle to survive.

It is enduring, this Last Love; it is a bulwark against the world; we take strength from it; and we return to it again and again as our one true refuge from the storms of life.

You are my Last Love.

You are the bright face in my dreams and the smile that lifts my heart.

You are the unwavering strength that carries me through life and the harbor in which I rest.

That First Love memory will never dim;
that Last Love harbor will ever endure.

But never think, My Love, that the gentle memories slip into quiet contentment. No My Love, those memories feed a raging fire.

First Love is a sweet questing,
but Last Love is a soul consuming passion.

I think My Love liked that story. I see now that it was so prophetic and that soul consuming passion ends not with awakening! I feel it for My Love yet, and I know I ever will.

My wish for you, Dear Reader, is that you feel it, too.

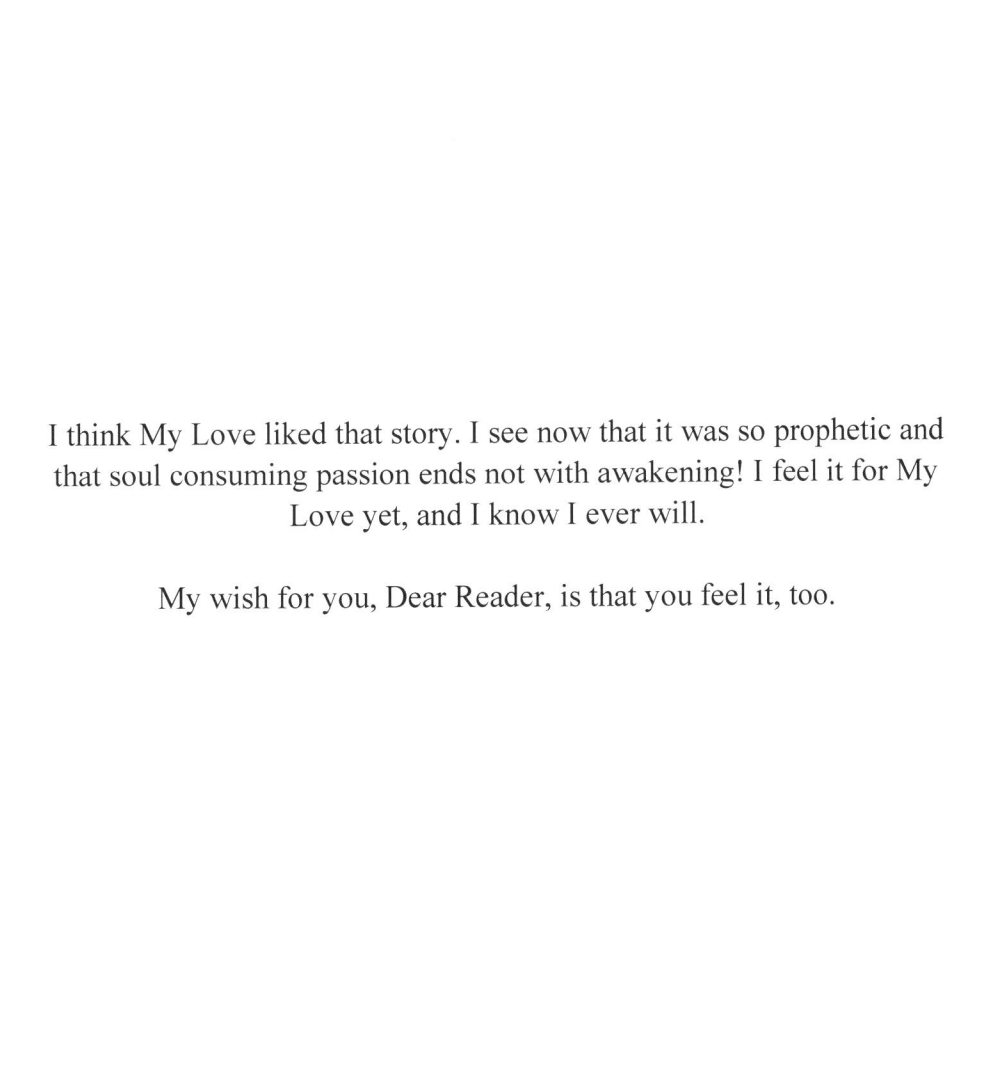

In the days following My Love's awakening, she began to speak to me. She was wroth with me because my poetry had turned dark. She bade me write a joyous poem, for our love was ever joyous.
This is what emerged.

I hope, Dear Reader, that your love is joyous.

Joy!

June bride, great joy, such bliss, such love, your kiss!
We wed, My Love, with words, we pledged our love!
True love, this is, no words describe this bliss!
We laugh, we dance, we sing, we kiss, My Love!

The sun doth shine, sweet breeze caress, our cheeks!
Your eyes do smile, your hand in mine, we run!
My heart is full, My Love, my life complete!
I am so blest! Rejoice, do I! I won!

So bright, filled with delight, future we give!
Please Time, stand still, please Time! For a life time!
Just us, we two, the world, it's ours, we live!
I hear a bell! For us, the earth doth chime!

Our love is true, I see! Leave me, never!
Forever! Love thee, I will, forever!

This came to me as I was selecting photographs for inclusion in the Celebration book that I prepared for My Love. I saw the only picture that we ever had from our first home.

Please remember, Dear Reader, that your home is in your love's heart, not in any building or place!

Home!

We're home, My Love, our home, My Love, this home!
Tis ours to love, to have, to live, such bliss!
First home, last home, my home, your home, our home!
Come bless this home, My Love, with this, your kiss!

Not this, these walls, these doors, this roof, but here!
Right here, in here, My Love, your heart, my heart!
Our home, My Love, is us, is we, to share!
Where e'er we be, nor manse, nor hut, ne'er part!

Content, My Love, with you, with now, so sweet!
To think, our lives art bound, no twain, but we!
I was but half, My Love, but now, complete!
I am, My Love, now home, My Love, with thee!

Nor storm, My Love, nor sea, nor miles, nor strife,
will keep, this heart from thee, My Love, My Wife!

Each time my thoughts turn dark, My Love whispers to me! Our days were filled with joy! Tell your readers! They must know that love means complete and utter joy!

Tis so, Dear Reader. My thoughts turn to a beautiful day in May when we drove our jeep through the mountains high. The sun was shining bright and the wind was in My Love's hair, and she laughed and smiled with every mile.

Try that, Dear Reader, with your love! Just go for a drive! Anywhere!

The Wind

We drove that day through hills untold, My Love!
Your smile so bright the sun did'st hide, tis true!
Your glance askance, your hair did'st dance, above!
Your laugh so sweet, my joy complete in you!

It rang in peals, your laugh, My Love, a gift!
To see your smile, your joy, your love replete!
The wind, My Love, it whipped, your face, so swift!
My mind did'st spin, I caught your joy, so sweet!

To watch the wind at play, your hair astray!
We laughed, we sang, the sun so warm, did'st shine!
Pure joy, My Love, more joy than I can say!
My heart is full, so thrilled, am I, you're mine!

The wind did'st kiss those cheeks, those eyes so bright!
I kissed them, too, My Love, my world aright!

Love seems so much richer when it is quietly shared. My Love and I were content to softly share a couch before the fire.

The simple joys are the best. Take time, Dear Reader, to share those joys with your love. Do it tonight.

Firelight

Shadows dark doth invite fire light to play!
I hold your hand, I watch fire light! Doth dance!
I'm blest, My Love, beyond what words can say!
Thou turns to kiss my lips! Fire lights thy glance!

We sit, we talk, art bathed in soft fire light!
We have no gold, My Love, we have no lands!
No need have we of more than this, so right!
The fire, My Love, doth warm our cheeks our hands!

Just this, to hold your hand, to be with you!
Fire light doth warm my heart and kiss your cheeks!
Tis all I want, tis all I need, my due!
Kiss me softly and make my life complete!

Content we are, to sit and touch, this night!
And watch the dance and play of this fire light!

JoAnn loved snow. She liked to watch it falling, she liked to walk in the softly falling flakes. I loved to watch her watch the flakes. Whenever it would snow, we would bundle up and walk through the flakes, hand in hand. These were some of the sweetest times. The snow muffled all sound, and it seemed that we were the only people on the entire planet! It seemed the snow was made for just us.

Dear Reader, take your love for a walk in the snow! Tis magical!

Snowflakes!

Snowflakes! Falling softly! Painting eyelashes!
We walk, hand in hand and the flakes drift down!
So quiet! Deep snow! Tis just a perfect path!
Nothing better! With thee and snow abounds!

No where to go! We're trapped by snow! So grand!
Just you and me, My Love, and flakes of snow!
This is just what I would have done, if planned!
You love this snow! I love just you! Storm blow!

Snowflakes! Falling upon your lovely face!
They kiss your lips! No, wait! I kiss your lips!
You laugh, I laugh! Such joy! We run! We race!
Tingles, My Love, from toes to fingertips!

Wading in snow so deep, house bound, are we!
Mem'ries are made of this! Just you and me!

My Love was never more beautiful than when she was pregnant. Of course, like all women, she would never believe that. She told me that she felt like a cow or some other strangely mammalian creature! But there is a glow about a woman when she carries a new life in her womb, a glow that draws every eye and makes every man swoon.

With Child!

I won't break, thee cried to me! Kiss me, Fool!
I did'st, My Love! I kissed thee well! I'm thrilled!
So beautiful thou art, My Love! Tis true!
And I, My Love, am perfectly fulfilled!

My babe, tis here! In awe, am I, of thou!
You glow, My Love! Light leaks from every pore!
So soft, you seem, tender and sweet, I vow!
And yet, so strong, you are! Strong as yon torr!

Art glorious, My Love! I cry, thee art!
Dost thou want a boy whispered thee to me!
I want your babe, My Love, our babe, My Heart!
A babe to love! Care not, be he or she!

Our babe! Made by our love! By thee and me!
Such love I have, for babe and thee! And thee!

As I approach this colossal job of trying to tell you, Dear Reader, of the love that JoAnn and I shared, I am reminded that thou dost not know of the years and their effect on our love. Well, the effect of the years was naught. Each year, our love was greater than before, despite what the hateful glass might show.

May it be so with you, Dear Reader, and your love!

Each Morn

Each morn, the sun and I doth kiss thy face!
That lovely face doth grace us both, thee smiles!
Each day I find, my love doth grow, apace!
How not, My Love! No matter, Love, the miles!

The years, they fly, like days, My Love, they do!
The glass, my face doth show, is now so gray!
I wish the sands full stop! Just let us woo!
The sands still fall, they will not stop their sway!

But warmth and love I feel, in your embrace!
My face, it matters not! My heart is yours!
Each year, a day it seems, I can'st keep pace!
But love, I know, I know it deep and pure!

Each morn, My Love, your face doth smile at me!
Nor sun, nor gloom, can dim that smile, My Thee!

My generation may be lost, Dear Reader! I do so wonder! I am not sure whether the young people of today have the slightest concept of what "making out" might mean. In our day, young couples would spend their evenings kissing. It was marvelous, to kiss your love for hours on end! The sweet embrace, the questing hands, the lips, the tongues, quite marvelous!

And then, sometimes, a young lady who was deeply in love with her gentleman might offer her breast to his mouth!
Oh, that, Dear Reader, was manna in the dessert!
It might seem so tame to the youth of today, but I do regret that they know not the thrill of those soft questings!

The soft and gentle things are always the best, Dear Reader!
Go offer thy breast to thy lover, Dear Reader! Do it now!

Making Out

Thy kiss, so sweet! Thy body soft! Excite!
I kiss thy face, thy cheeks, thy eyes! So sweet!
I love thee, so! Thee knows it's so! Aright!
To hold thee so, and hear thy heart! Complete!

And then, My Love, thee offers me, thy breast!
I cup thy breast, I kiss thy breast! Divine!
So tender, thee! So soft, so sweet! Art blessed!
So soft thee art! I love thee so! Art mine!

My mind doth spin, my heart's afire! Such bliss!
Content, am I, to kiss thee so! Thy breast!
Tis magical, to hold thee close, and kiss!
So beautiful, thou art, my heart, arrest!

My heart doth race! My mouth on thine! Sublime!
Thy heart doth race! Thy mouth on mine! Divine!

In many ways, older lovers become more comfortable. Or, at least, we did. I learned how exactly to make My Love smile, to make her sigh.

Be not persuaded, Dear Reader, that passion fades. It does not! Our passion grew apace with the years. She could give me a certain glance and turn my loins to fire!

But the quiet moments grow richer. Just sitting together, talking about our day and holding hands became the single most important thing that we could do each day.

Take time to do that, Dear Reader, with your love, tonight.

Growing Older

A comfort be, My Love, in growing old!
Tis true! My love for you will stronger be!
The days, the years, they matter not, nor cold!
Each day doth bring us closer, me to thee!

So content, holding hands on endless walks!
Soft days, soft nights, they slip on by like ghosts!
Yes content, holding hands through endless talks!
And friendly days and friendly nights, so close!

Passion still, yes tis real, undimmed by time!
Thy kiss still burns, embrace inflames! Burns high!
And love remains undimmed by years unkind!
And now, dost know thee well, can'st make thee sigh!

So, love is sweet when youths doth meet, no rue!
But love is grand when grey heads plan, tis true!

It seemed that where ever we went, we drew the eyes of strangers. JoAnn would tell me it was because we were a striking couple, all dressed in black, and me with my Stetson hat! But, we both knew that was not the magnet for the eyes.

If you watch, Dear Reader, and observe, you will see so few couples strolling hand in hand, where ere you go, whose love blazes like the sun. That was us, Dear Reader! Anyone could see our love! Everyone could see our love! To see love like ours doth arrest the eyes! People will look, and then they will smile! It's just the power of love!

You can do it, too, Dear Reader! Take your love's hand, and let your love come into your eyes as you gaze at your love. Passers by will stop and stare! I promise thee!

Drawing Eyes

You often say, we catch the eyes, of passers by, My Love.
You think it me, I think it you, but eyes doth stray, to us!
Your dress I think, you think it mine! But that can'st be, My Love!
We are just we! Just you and me! Celebrity! Not us!

What can'st it be? What draws the eyes? To thee and me? No clue?
I tell thee true! I know just why, the eyes do stray! Tis love!
They see our love! It glows and glows! It beckons all! Tis true!
Such love is rare! It draws the eye! It warms the heart, My Love!

We can'st not hide, the way we feel! Tis there for all, to see!
Thee hold my hand, thee glance at me! Tis plain to see! Your love!
I smile at thee, can'st help it not! Nor thee, My love! Tis we!
We are in love, our watchers see! They envy us, My Love!

I wish that they, had love like ours! Could know this bliss, thy kiss!
Ignore them, Love! Come here to me! Come taste my lips, my kiss!

JoAnn loved our children with complete, total abandon, utterly, totally, impossibly! I think that a man can never truly understand the love a woman feels for a babe she has carried under her heart before she carries it in her arms.

But, I can tell you this, Dear Reader! To watch your love gaze into your child's angelic face is magical. Simply magical.

Mother's Love

I watch thee, Love, with this our babe! So dear!
Cradled in love, just so sweetly, is he!
To gaze upon this face of love, so near,
doth fill my heart and soul with love for thee!

I love this babe, my son! Oh so fiercely!
A part of me, a part of you, he is!
A perfect love, thee gives! Oh so dearly!
My cup is full, my son, My Love, oh tis!

And yet, to see, a mother's love, tis sweet!
Thou clasps him close, My Love, to keep him safe!
A mother's love, tis soft and strong, complete!
He sleeps and stirs, My Love, in love's embrace!

Thy face, My Love, thy gaze, they capture me!
To see such love, such grace! Oh, I love thee!

I always called My Love, Sweetheart. From our earliest days together that diminutive just rolled from my tongue and it would always evoke a smile from My Love. It evokes a smile from me now, as I remember those beautiful smiles with which she graced me.

She was and is my Sweetheart and I love and miss her fiercely.

Go and embrace your love, Dear Reader, embrace your love fiercely!

Sweetheart!

Sweetheart! Doth I call thee, for I love thee!
My love is vast! My love is deep! Sweetheart!
Sweetheart, my sweet, I cry, dost thou love me?
I cry my love, I shout it clear! Ne'er part!

You fill my heart with this, your sweet embrace!
I hold your hand, My Love, you hold my heart!
You fill my mind with this, your loving glance!
For this and all thy gifts I cry, Sweetheart!

Simple, it tis, Sweetheart, my name for you!
But must I smile, to speak it you, Sweetheart!
And give me back a smile or two, you do!
I call thee true! My name for you! My heart!

We walk through days, thy hand in mine, Sweetheart!
No more can'st ask, I need just this, Sweetheart!

It takes but a smile, it takes but a glance from your true love to set your heart afire, Dear Reader. I know this truly!

Watch your love, Dear Reader, and never miss that glance. When it comes you must go to your love. Never wait!

Your Glance

You glance at me, you glance away and smile!
I know that glance! It strikes a fire in me!
You know this, Love, you do! You've known the while!
I love your glance, I love thee, too, just thee!

Your love, it pours, from brown eyes pours, your glance!
You pour on me, your love so warm, so free!
So blest, I am, to hold your hand, and dance!
So pure, your love, so sweet! Will ever be!

Come heed this fire, My Love! Come tame this flame!
Your cooling touch, your soothing hand, I crave!
I feel your heart! It beats with mine! Aflame!
Our hearts beat fast, My Love! A tidal wave!

And now, this glance! I know it well! Takes wing!
A glance so full of love for me, I sing!

I remember many perfect days with My Love. It could be sunshine or rain, so long as she smiled at me, it was the same!
Those days slipped far too fast through the hourglass of time, and years seemed to pass like days. As long as My Love clasped my hand, I just did not care!

Go take your love's hand, Dear Reader! The single most powerful statement of love that exists, Dear Reader, is to take thy love's hand!

Perfect Day!

A golden day this was, My Love! So bright!
A perfect day, twas this, My Love! Tis true!
A lovely day, and lit by magic light!
A gentle day, so sweet and pure, with you!

We walked and talked, your hand in mine, twas fine!
We planned and thought, the week to be, and all!
Just us, we two, the world stood still, in time!
The sands, they flow! Can'st stop them not! They fall!

But days like this, My Love, need just thy kiss!
A golden sun, a walk with thee, My Sweet!
Can'st spend my days, my life, my years like this!
So long as I, can'st hold your hand! Complete!

The years doth fly, I don't care why, with thee!
It matters not, My Love, for I love thee!

One of the great joys of my life was working together with My Love. We had a traditional marriage for eight years, making our living apart. But that was always so unsatisfying. I needed more time with her. Finally, we were able to share a career. When we finished school, we taught together. We shared an office at school and an office at home. We wrote together, we plied our minds together through our research, we did everything together. All of this, side by side.

We had a little routine. We had our music playing softly in the background all the time. When the song we called ours would play, we would stop what we were doing, and share an embrace while the song played. Looking back now, I just wish the song would have played a little more often.

Don't miss a chance to share an embrace with your love, Dear Reader! Take advantage of every opportunity!

Working Together

To hear your thoughts, to list your mind, tis joy!
To work with you, to build with you, divine.
We make our way, we earn our bread, employ!
We build so well, so strong, your mind with mine!

Tis just we two, we think and scheme, we do!
Tis all the more, and powerful, we call.
Because our minds, our bodies one, we rule!
Tis sweet this work, because we share, it all.

We choose our path, we guide our ship, we two.
Tis thee and me, the world entire, we share.
We wend our way, through sea and cliff, we do!
My partner, thee, in life and love, how rare!

My friend thou art, my lover, too! My wife!
I love thee true and share with you, my life!

Ever and anon people would ask us about spending so much time together. How can you both work and live together, they would say. People seemed to be surprised at our desire to always be together. We actually never found an answer for that question. To us, it was simply natural to always want to be together. We worked better together, we played better together, everything was better, together. We did not know why other people thought that strange.

Looking back now, my regrets are all about the time we did not spend together. And, I now realize that nothing is more precious than the time you spend with your true love. It need not be anything more than simply sharing the silence of a summer's eve. Together is where true lovers belong.

Choose time together with your love, Dear Reader. Time and more time, Dear Reader! There can never be enough.

Together

Together, Love. How powerful, that phrase.
Tis all I want, to ever be, with thee.
We make our way, through this life, our way.
I never tire, watching your face, just thee.

To be apart, sweet sorrow not, tis pain.
When duty calls, and part we must, tis fell.
How long before, we're together, again?
Tis far too long, till time is up, ring bell!

I want to be, My Love, right here with thee.
Let's part no more, together be, tis bliss.
I want to share, My Love, eternity.
And all I want, and all I need, your kiss!

Together, Love! For that and all, I long!
Together, Love, is where we doth belong

Passion was always there between us. It was just below the surface. A glance, a touch, could ignite it like a fire. Young lovers may think that passion fades. But, Dear Reader, it fades not!

I loved being with My Love, I loved talking with My Love, I loved working with My Love. I loved just holding her hand and listening to the silence. And, I loved making love with My Love.

Make love with your love, Dear Reader! Do it tonight!

Your Embrace

Thou thrills me still, My Love, with thine embrace.
Thee touches me, with sure intent, and skill.
I burn with fire, My Love, my heart doth race!
Thee bends my mind, my body sings! And will!

Each time we love, tis like our first, tis true!
To lie with thee, to be with thee, desire!
Each time we touch, My Love, it tis anew!
This touch will end, thy touch doth end, in fire!

How can'st we tire, of love like this? Kiss me!
Our hearts aflame, our passion builds! Higher!
I come to thee, to quench thy fire! Kiss thee!
Come lie with me, My Love, and quench my fire!

To kiss your lips, to list' your heart, with mine!
Thee body sings! My body sings! To thine!

I loved to make my My Love laugh. Her laughter was infectious and each time I managed to twist a phrase, she would smile and laugh and I would have to laugh with her. She loved subtle humor, a play on words, a clever repartee. She spared not a smile for broad or base comedy, but it seemed that I could always find that smile. No matter what the day held, no matter the task, her smile would brighten my world and make my day.

Laugh with your love, Dear Reader! Laugh every day!

Laughter!

I heard you laugh, my spirts rose, My Dear!
That's all it takes, My Love, to make my day!
I love that laugh, I love thee, too, tis clear!
You laugh and smile, it helps me find my way!

I share a pun, I twist a phrase, for you!
You laugh at me, you smile at me, delight!
I try and try, to make you laugh, tis true!
I crave that smile, that dear, dear smile, so bright!

Tis drink for me, and meat for me, your laugh!
Our days are filled, filled with joy and laughter!
Our laughter, Dear, My Dear, smooths this our path!
Laughter, My Dear, helps us, joy to capture!

You laugh, you smile, my heart is filled with thee!
I laugh and smile, and then you smile at me!

How does one tell that one's love is true? Oh, true love is rare, or so
I'm told, but powerful. Your true love gives, and gives and gives.
Never takes, never needs, just gives. Not wealth, not gold, no the gift
of true love is far greater. The gift of true love is one's total self.
And the giving of that gift is life changing.

Give your love that gift, Dear Reader. Do it tonight. Not just your
body, but your heart and mind and self. Give it all.

True Love

To find thy love, to kiss thy love, tis bliss!
Heaven doth note, the sky doth sigh, for thee!
True love is rare, it shakes the world, that kiss!
It calls for you, it calls for all, and me!

How can we tell, when true love calls, asks thee?
No doubt have we, tis clear as clear, it calls.
It is the gift, the gift of love, you see.
It never takes, it only gives, gives all.

The gift of all, withholding naught, tis fell!
Expecting naught, to give thine all, tis this.
The gift of love, of self, is powerful!
Nor gold, nor myrrh, no wealth can buy, this gift.

My love gave me, herself entire, herself.
Myself entire, I gave to her, myself.

Whether rich or poor, the greatest gift that lovers give each other is themselves. To lose yourself in making love with your lover is simply divine. Each time we made love, I lost myself in My Love, and she in me. Nothing existed in the world in that moment but we two and nothing was more important than giving joy to each other.

Dear Reader, don't miss an opportunity to make love with your love! Read these words to your love and make sweet love with your love!
Do it tonight!

Making Love

I burn for thee! I yearn for thee! Such need,
I have for thee! Come lie with me! Need thee!
Make love to me! My heart's afire! I plead,
Come quench my fire, with thy soft touch! Kiss me!

Thy glance, thine eyes, they strike a fire! Doth burn!
Come lie with me, and hold me close! Embrace!
Thy body soft, embrace so sweet! I yearn!
I kiss thy lips, thy body, too! Heart race!

I love the touch, the feel of thee! Desire!
Your mouth on mine! I drink thee in! Like wine!
My hands on thee, thy hands on me! Tis fire!
To softly touch! To gently kiss! Divine!

Make love with me, I love thee so! Art mine!
As we entwine, my heart, my mind, art thine!

My Love just loved teddy bears. All shapes and sizes and types and colors. I bought her hundreds of them over the years. We traveled a great deal with our work, and I always tried to find a teddy bear in every city. She loved them, but I loved giving them.

No matter how many bears she had, each new one would evoke a sweet, sweet smile, and a thank you kiss. Oh, how I yearn for that smile and that kiss!

Dear Reader, don't forget the smile and the kiss! No matter the gift, always give your love your smile and your kiss!

Teddy Bears

This teddy bear, it tis for thee! Cuddly!
Tis joy to watch, thy face alight! To see!
Thee clasps it tight! Thee strokes its fur! Lovely!
A simple toy, this teddy bear! For thee!

I know, I know, I gave before! And more!
I just can't stop, I love to watch, your eyes!
Each time I give, a teddy bear, adore!
I just adore, the smile you give, the cry!

Each bear doth earn, a smile so sweet, and bright!
The sun doth hide! Cannot compete, with thee!
My world complete, thy smile doth make, aright!
Tis not the bear, that earns your smile, tis me!

My just reward, thou dost bestow, a kiss!
And that, My Love, reward enough! Thy kiss!

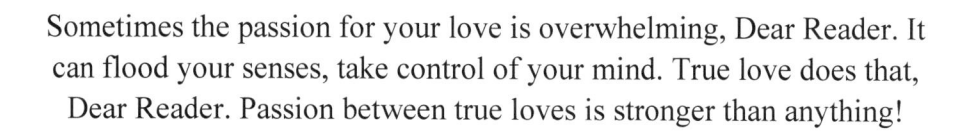

Sometimes the passion for your love is overwhelming, Dear Reader. It can flood your senses, take control of your mind. True love does that, Dear Reader. Passion between true loves is stronger than anything!

When you feel that passion, Dear Reader, you must go to your love! You must love your love! Make love to your love!

That's what true lovers do!

Passion

Please come to me, thou sayest me, doth cry!
I need thee, Love, I want thee, Love, thy touch!
My mouth on thine, thy breasts, thy thighs, thee sighs!
I want thee, Love, I need thee, Love, so much!

Thy touch doth burn, I crave the burn, I cry!
Thy lips on mine, I clasp thee tight! Embrace!
My mind hath fled, so lost am I, I sigh!
So lost in you, I kiss your lips, your face!

Passion so great, doth drive the mind, the heart!
My passion soars, My Love! My heart doth burst!
Thee must come, Love, come to me, Love, ne'er part!
I love thee so, I want to be, immersed!

Make love with me! My passion grows, I plead!
Immersed in thee, entwined with thee, I need!

My Love loved summers. She loved winters and springs and falls, as well, of course. But summers had a special appeal. The crickets singing to their loves, the velvet black of a summer's eve, twas magical. We were just content to sit together and listen to the night. That black velvet calls to lovers, Dear Reader!

I think what I miss most is sitting with My Love, holding her hand, and listening to the quiet.

Don't miss that, Dear Reader! Don't miss it! Go hold your love's hand tonight and introduce your love to the quiet!

Summer's Eve

To sit with thee, on summer's eve, and list!
To sit with thee, and hold thy hand, so sweet!
List to quiet, list to the night, just list!
In silence be, my heart is full, complete!

I need not more, my life fulfilled, by this!
Companions, Dear, and lovers, too, art we!
I doth need more! Just one thing more! Thy kiss!
Kiss me softly. Kiss me sweetly, My Thee!

To sit like this, with my true love, God's bless!
Your hand in mine, your heart in mine, my wish!
The world is ours, this night divine! Art blessed!
The quiet sings, the night's alive, for us!

I hear your heart. It beats with mine, My Love!
You hear my heart. It beats with thine, My Love!

I woke at the keyboard at 3:30 AM on August 17, two days after My Love awakened. I was naked, cold, and drunk. I was disoriented and took several minutes to realize who and where I was. When I could see, this poem was on the screen.
I do not remember writing a single word of it.

I warn thee, Dear Reader, tis raw!

Awake!

Weep not, My Dear, for me, My Dear, no tears.
No words, nor tears, nor thoughts, can me, console.
My Love doth wake, my heart doth break, I fear.
I dream, I sleep, to wake, I yearn, my soul.

This life is but a dream, I know, I fear.
Wake me, My Love, wake me, My Dear, awake!
No dream can be as sweet to me, no tears!
Dream not, but wake I would, my soul, please take!

The world, we owned, the keys were ours, we roared!
We dreamed so deep, My Love, you dreamt with me!
The sky, the sun, the stars, were ours, we soared!
Sweet was this dream, My Love, when shared with thee.

But now, My Love, you wake, My Love, and fly!
Must I, now dream, My love, alone, but why!

My Love truly loved making love with me, it was very clear. Always, she wanted me to be gentle, so very gentle and soft, and slow. She liked to feel the passion grow and it thrilled me so to watch it, and feel it myself. A feather touch, a soft kiss just so, and the fire builds.

Dear Reader, thee needs make love to your love like this! Read these words to your love, and make love to your love like this tonight!

Gentle

Be soft thy touch, gentle thy lips, My Love!
My body sings! It sings to thee! Be slow!
Oh, gently be, thy hands need be, My Love!
Thy mouth on mine, thy hands strike fire! Be slow!

These sweet, sweet words, thee sayest me, My Love!
Slowly, softly, make love to me, thee pleads!
Softly, slowly, and gentle be, My Love!
My passion grows! Make love with me, I plead!

Thy gentle hand and thy sweet mouth doth sing!
They sing to me, they kindle me, strike fire!
So sweet this love, when gentle be, doth sing!
I love this love, so softly be, but fire!

So soft art thee, so tender be, My Love!
Must gently be, my hands on thee, My Love!

I wrote this for JoAnn on June 12, 2012. It was our 41st wedding anniversary. She was hospitalized at the time, and I was sleeping in her room. We planned to do something for our anniversary later, when she felt better. We wanted to take a trip, perhaps back to Gatlinburg, Tennessee, where we spent the three days of our honeymoon in 1971, the first nights we ever spent together. She never felt better, and we never took that trip.

Don't put off things, Dear Reader, take your love and do them now!

Why Thee I Love

Your kiss, first kiss, this kiss doth shake the earth, the sky, My Love.
And yet, and still, you ask me why,
oh why, should I, thee love?

Your love doth bless my days, my nights,
my life, with grace, My Love.
I'm blessed, by sweet caress, by soft embrace,
so I, thee love.

Your world, it drums, it doth tattoo,
with mystery, My Love.
That gift, a glimpse, a sight, of sweet fairy,
so I, thee love.

Two sons, you bore, so bright, so strong,
and taught to soar, My Love.
Great pride, they bring, these two tercels;
these tigers roar,
so I, thee love.

You taught, you found, ideas so rare,
to guide my days, My Love.
The gifts you gave, strike fire; my mind ablaze,
so I, thee love.

Writer, leader, partner, helper,
my safe harbor, My Love.
My source of strength, anchor, hearth and lover,
so I, thee love.

You see so far, you fly so high,
you share your gift, My Love.
I see so far, I fly so high, from your uplift,
so I, thee love.

We climbed so high, we led, tis true,
we dared so much, My Love.
But all we did, I know, tis from your touch,
so I, thee love.

A team, we are, not two, but one,
one heart, one mind, My Love.
So strong, we are, so fierce; our lives entwined,
so I, thee love.

You are my source of joy; my life,
you justify, My Love.
And yet, and still, I ask you why,
oh why, should you, me love?

Oh no, because we two are one,
one mind, I know, My Love!
It's clear that we were born to love,
we both must know, My Love.

We know because, that kiss, this kiss,
doth shake the earth, each kiss!
Our days enriched, our lives fulfilled,
our love's rebirth, each kiss.

So I, thee love, must love, do love, will love, always, forever.
And you, must you, me love, will love, always, forever.

Those words bring me such pain when I read them now. They are so pale beside the burning, raging fire that was and is our love. My gift of words is so slight, I fear, that I can never paint the love we share.

I hope that you, Dear Reader, can share a love like ours.

My Love was perfectly gorgeous, of course. Here is a shot I snapped at one of our rare visits to the Beach. I think this was 1979, and our boys would have been four and six. We stayed in a tiny little bungalow with walls as thin as paper. Her tousled hair and come hither smile still lights my fire today! This is one of my favorite pictures and this is how I see her in my dreams. I dream of her every night and that taste of salt doth haunt my dreams!

Dear Reader, while thou can'st, don't dream of your love! Go to your love! Make love to your love! Put a little salt upon your lips, then kiss your love! Love your love! Now! Tonight! Don't forget the salt!

A Taste of Salt

The wind and sand, the surf, the sun, illume!
Thee taste of salt, thy lips art chapped! The taste!
Thy so sweet smile, thy tousled hair, inflame!
Make love to me, oh, sweet my love! Let's haste!

Be soft, My Love, quiet must be! Kiss me!
Tis hard, My Love, to quiet be! Need shout!
Don't wake the boys, My Love! Be quiet, thee!
Hush be, My Love! The boys wilt wake! No doubt!

I wilt, My Love, so quiet be! But thee!
Just took my mind, my senses be! Tis true!
I need thee, Love! I want thee, Love! Just me!
That taste of salt, upon thy lips, I rue!

My Love, thou art, desire enfleshed, art thee!
The sea, the sand, the taste of salt! Love thee!

It seemed that where ever we went, people watched us. My Love thought that we made a striking couple. She even thought me handsome, though that must have been her limited vision. She told me once that she felt blest that people could see us holding hands while she clutched a giant stuffed elephant as we walked in Las Vegas. She said that she felt a queen, walking by my side, when all knew that my heart was hers. My heart was hers, was true! But she, a king, made me, tis true! We ever dressed so carefully. Never would we appear in casual or unlovely clothes. We dressed each day as though the opera we would attend. My Love insisted that ne'er would we appear in jeans or in flats. To step into the world, she insisted that we would be dressed to impress! Add to that, that we truly did make an eye catching couple because our love was palpable. It seemed that every eye we caught and every heart we strummed.

Dress carefully, Dear Reader! Never casual be! Not even at home! My Love dressed for me each day. Never would she even think about being casual or untidy. She dressed for me, and when the world saw her, they saw a beautiful woman who held my hand.

Dress for your love, Dear Reader! Dress just so!

Catching Eyes

My Love did'st think, a handsome guy, was I.
Twas never so, distinctive yes, but she!
Twas her sweet face, that drew the eye, oh my!
Tis true that folks, did'st look at us, just we!

They thought that we, a couple made, tis true!
Our love was clear, to every eye, and heart!
I care'st not, for prying eyes! Love you!
They all could'st see, how close we are, ne'er part!

Tis rare to see, true lovers stroll, in hand!
Our hands in hands, our hearts so clear, art we!
All heads doth turn, as we stroll past, no plan!
True love dost glow, so all wilt know! Tis we!

A glow we hath, tis love they see, in we!
Can'st help it not, our love doth glow, My Thee!

This came to me among a number of others during the days following My Love's awakening. I think this might have been August 20, or so. I drank a lot in those days, and my days and nights got very confused.

Again, Dear Reader, this is raw.

My Pain

Always and forever, that's what you would say to me!
Always and forever, that's what I would say to thee!
Always and forever, for our love was meant to be!

I wonder how many lifetimes I have loved thee.
Could it be ten thousand years? I think it must be.
But ten thousand more will not be enough for me.

Why have we been parted? We can not be parted!
You are here beside me. We can not be parted!
We are not two, but one. We can not be parted!

Why does my heart yet beat? Why does my blood yet flow?
I yearn to be with thee, where and when thou dost go!
When can I come to thee? Soon I hope, you must know!

There are miles I must tread. People I must care for.
They hold me. They bind me. You love them. That and more.
Tasks that be, will be done. Time please fly, I implore.

I feel your lips on mine, I love you, my Sweetheart!
This will be a moment, I thought it, my Sweetheart!
I feel your lips on mine, I love you, my Sweetheart!

But you woke! You woke while I yet dreamed! Thee, Thee, Thee!
I thought no! Not to us! God would not! Not to me!
I was wrong. You did wake! Now I dream, come to me!

Dream of life. So sad and yet so strange. Yearn to wake.
We should all yearn to wake. Pray thee my soul to take.
With thee I would be, Love! If I wake! Let me wake!

Always and forever, your kiss doth shake the earth!
Come to me! I to thee! I care not, for this earth!
Duty binds! I am wroth! I need thee! Not this earth!

I love thee! Thee loves me! This I know! Know it still!
Together, we will be. Soon, be soon! This I will!
Yearn to wake! This I do! Wake to you! Know I will!

Always and forever, that's what you would say to me!
Always and forever, that's what I would say to thee!
Always and forever, for our love was meant to be!

I remember feeling such pain that duty kept me here, yet dreaming. My Love gave me tasks to perform to secure the future for our sons, and bade me promise to see those done before I followed her. I so wanted to go with her! I still do! As the poets say, death is light as a feather, but duty is as heavy as a mountain. Oh, tis true!

I loved to kiss, My Love, tis true. She loved to kiss me, too. We'd start each day with a kiss or two, and end each nigh with kisses, too. I could never get enough of the feel of her lips on mine. Our world started with kisses when we were just children driving around in a jeep. Our world ended with a kiss. I kissed her moments before she awakened. I would give my soul to kiss her now.

Dear Reader, miss not a chance to kiss thy love! Each morn, each eve, each time you greet, each time you leave your love! Kiss your love!

Do it now! Go kiss your love! Right now! For me!

Kisses

Did'st greet each day, with thy sweet kiss, did'st thee!
Twas my reward, for loving thee, that kiss!
Did'st greet each eve, with that sweet kiss, did'st we!
I needed that, to close my day, thy kiss!

My days and nights, have fled like mice, to holes!
That kiss, so sweet, my day did'st greet, I cry!
The years have fled, I know not where, I'm old!
So sweet, that kiss, my day did'st end, I sigh!

The years are light, upon my back, but thee!
Without thy kiss, the sun can'st light, my way!
Without thy kiss, the moon doth hide, from me!
Thy kiss must start, thy kiss must end, each day!

I feel thee, Love, in my poor heart, but Love!
I miss that kiss! I miss that kiss, My Love!

I loved My Love's face. I loved her body. I loved her soul. But, most of all, I loved her mind. She has the most incredible mind! If you have read the Celebration Book I wrote, you know how incredible she was. If you have not, find it, please, at www.JoAnnCarland.com.

We were scholars, you know, Dear Reader. We were known as the Doctors Carland, and our academic fame was truly vast. We became among the best known scholars in our field in all of the world. All of that, and all of the accolades that followed, were a result of JoAnn's mind. We meshed so well. She would see a connection in the discrete bits of data and information we were studying, and tell it to me. I would see yet another linkage beyond, and tell it to her. She would see the final linkage, and we would know a new thing! A thing no one had known before! It was magical. Just magical. And, the greatest thing was not the fame. It was simply learning together.

Forget not your mind, Dear Reader, in your relationship with your love! Your body is powerful, Dear Reader, and it sings to your love, but your mind is more powerful! Talk with your love! Think with your love! Mesh minds with your love! Tis magical!

Her Mind

Yes, Love, tis right! I see that, too! Tis clear!
To work with thee, to learn with thee, divine!
Thy mind so sharp! Thee see so far! No peer!
No peer hath thee, no peer hath we! Art mine!

Thy mind to mine! My mind to thine! My thee!
We see so well, we master all! Compel!
We write so fast, to make this last, doth we!
This great insight! Tis ours, it tis! So fell!

Our star doth rise, on this our work! Tis true!
We make our mark, on this our field! Insight!
Success have we, and fame have we! Thank you!
But joy we have! In finding truth! Art right!

So blest are we! Our minds doth mesh! My Love!
So blest am I! To work with thee, My Love!

My Love loved to make love in the mornings. We would rise and
bathe and come back together in joy.
Nights are wonderful and evenings are grand, but nothing compares to
making love in the morning.

Try this, Dear Reader! I promise thee a greater joy! Read these words
to your love! Make love with your love in the morning!

Mornings!

Tis morning, Love! Thee look so bright, and coy!
I touch thy hair, I kiss thy lips! So sweet!
I see that glance! I know that look, of joy!
Thee wants me, Love! And I want thee! Such heat!

Make love with me! My Love please do, I plead!
The sun doth kiss, our naked cheeks! So bright!
My tongue doth trace, these so sweet curves! I need!
I need thee, Love! I want thee, Love! Aright!

To make this love, in sunbeams bright! Delight!
The sun doth play, on cheeks and breasts! Thy face!
This morning love, it tis so sweet! And right!
My body sings! I love thee, Love! Hearts race!

The sun doth greet, our love anew! My Love!
These mornings make, our days so sweet! My Love!

A so funny tale is in my mind. My Love must be remembering this day. When the boys were little, four and six, and we had virtually no money, we decided to take them fishing. We went to one of those trout ponds where they charge you for each fish you catch. We thought, how many fish can they catch? They're just little boys!

Well, they caught and caught! Every time they cast their lines, they caught a fish! We got concerned, so we moved them to another spot. The fish won't bite here we thought. But, they did! The other people at the lake began to follow us around as we moved from spot to spot, trying to find a place where the boys could not catch a fish! Those people had not luck, but the boys could not miss! Finally, in a fit of desperation, JoAnn distracted the boys, and I dumped the rest of the bait into the pond!

When we cashed out with the owner, it came to $22.00. I had $25.00 in my pocket, and we had enough money left to buy gas to get home. The boys never had a better day, nor did we!

Children are such a blessing, Dear Reader! I cherish this memory! Spend some time, Dear Reader, cherishing your own memories!

Fishing

I can'st believe, thou criest me! The fish!
The boys just do, keep catching fish! Must stop!
How can'st we stop! Their joy so great! They wish!
I know, I know, But, Love, the cost! Must stop!

Let's move them, Love! Another spot! No fish!
That place just there. It looks so bare! Tis safe!
You've moved them, Love! Five times anon! Still fish!
They catch them here, they catch them there! Vouchsafe!

I know, My Love! The bait, let's lose! Can't fish!
Be careful, Love! Don't let them see! Don't look!
Do turn thy back, and shield me love! Here fish!
Please eat this bait, and bite thee not, their hooks!

Tis time to go, and clean these fish, My Sons!
Let's take our catch, and set our sights, for home!

Deep was my anger. I felt My Love aching for me just beyond this veil, and I knew that she felt the same pain as I from this separation. I so wanted to know why. This dark piece came to me on August 31st, some days after My Love awakened.

Answer, God!

Must I live! Should I die! Answer, God! Thee owes me!
Tell me, God! Live, then why? Answer, God! Speak to me!
Grown, my sons. Done, my work. Gone, my Love. Speak to me!
Dust, this life. Worth, I've none. No sunrise speaks to me!

I should die. Join my Love. Find my peace. Think Thee not?
What is left? Years of fear? Sickness, doubt? I think not!
I should go. Years of pain, I avoid. Think Thee not?
Simple step. Life to death. Find my Love. Say why not!

God is mute! Speak, My Love! Must I live! Should I die?
Come to thee! That I would! Nothing here! Can I die?
Miles to go. That I know. Soon will end. Then, I die?
Sleep, I would. Tired, I am. With thee, be! I should die!

Answer, not. Not from thee. Not from God. Not to me.
Need, I have. Answer, please! Torture, this! Answer me!

My Love was teaching High School in Asheville, North Carolina, when we married and I was stationed in Louisville, Kentucky, as a recruiting officer. She quit to move with me, but no sooner than we arrived in Louisville, we found that the Marine Corps was releasing me as an early discharge as part of their overall cutback. Suddenly, we were both unemployed!

Money was very tight. We learned about Ramen Noodles, and we struggled mightily! I got a job as a commissioned salesman, but she could not find a teaching job. She got some substitute teaching gigs, but that was all. I was a completely incompetent salesman! But never, ever, ever, did we regret anything! We had each other, and that was all we needed! Once in a while, we got a dollar ahead, and we would go to McDonald's for dinner. I learned to love those little hamburgers! But most of all, I loved My Love! No matter how dire things seemed to be, she always had a smile for me! I do so miss those smiles!

Please, Dear Reader, fail not to smile at your love! No matter the day, no matter the challenge, smile at your love! Always smile!

Smiles

Thee smile dost light, it lights my day, Sweetheart!
I so thee love, that smile so bright! Tis fierce!
Thee greet me with, that smile and kiss, My Heart!
I worry not! I have thy love! Thy kiss!

I know not how, this day will go, nor care!
I know just this, I love thee true! Tis true!
We make our way, through challenge great, beware!
But hand in hand, our heads held high, we rule!

Tis naught we need. We have each thee, the while!
Nor gold, nor myrrh, nor manse nor lands, have we!
I love thee so, please kiss me, Love! And smile!
For wealth I have! My pearl so great! Tis thee!

Our love prevails! Our love survives! Please smile!
What else can'st be! To set me free! Thy smile!

I found a childish diary among My Love's things. She had kept it but sporadically from the ages of 13 through 15. Oh, I am so sure she was laughing as I read. It was filled with declarations of love for first one young boy, then another. Sometimes, only a week apart! But this little poem was written inside the back cover, and it was in My Love's hand. She penned this early in 1964. She would have been fifteen.

Cherry Pink

It's cherry pink and apple blossom white when your true love comes your way.

It's cherry pink and apple blossom white, the poets say.

The story goes that once a cherry tree beside an apple tree did grow.

There a boy once met his bride to be, long, long ago.

He looked into her eyes, the breeze joined in the sighs!

I was so highly blest in my dream of life. It was absolutely perfect in every way in every day. Until My Love awakened.
This came to me on August 21st.

Blest and Curst!

Bles'sed am I, above all men, for thou dost love,
thou love'est me!
Me, only me! Thou love'est me! I shout your name!
I cry, I sing!
Great is the gift, that God gave me! I know not why!
God gave me thee!
To have and hold! God gave me thee! I sing, I dance!
Thee took my ring!

A'curst am I, above all men, for God did'st take,
took thee from me!
Forlorn am I, above all men! I cry, I shout!
I curse, I die!
But why, oh God! What sin was mine! To make Thee take,
my love to Thee!
How great this loss! The greatest gift, Thou took from me!
I ask Thee why!

No answer, God! I know not why! When all I did, was love Your gift!
I loved her true! With all my heart! With all my soul!
I loved her, God!
I love her still! I always will! To be so blest, then left bereft!
I feel her kiss! Upon my lips! Thee smote me, God! I curse that rod!

I know, I know! The sin is mine! I should rejoice!
I love thee still!
Thou wilt be mine! Thou art still mine! Thou loves me still!
Thee always will!

But each time, my pen flowed dark, My Love would whisper in my ear. Rejoice, My Love, she would say. This came to me hard on the heels of that last sonnet. My Love promised me that we would share our first kiss again.

Dear Reader, don't wait. Go share a kiss with your love.
Do it now!

First Kiss, Last Kiss

First kiss! The earth did shake! Earthquake! Tis' true!
You shook my life, My Love, My heart, My Soul!
Shook me, thou did'st, My Love, My Heart! Who knew!
Thou did'st, My Love, love me, love me! Was whole!

That kiss, my lips, were burnt, My Love! Art still!
It led, My Love, to life, My Heart, complete!
Love thee! Love me! We do, My Love, and will!
Our lives, our fates, entwined! Art now! So sweet!

Last kiss! Your lips! So soft! So sweet! Earthquake!
I thought, how sweet, that touch, My Love, such bliss!
My world did'st end, My Love! My heart, doth break!
You woke, My Love! My kiss, art now, last kiss!

So sweet, the first! So sweet, the last! I wen!
There must! There hast to be! First kiss! Again!

I penned this for My Love on Christmas Day, 1995. It seems such doggerel now. It was such a weak expression of the love I felt then and the love I feel now. Somehow, I think My Love saw through the words and into my heart. I know she sees it clearly now.

Why Do I Love Thee?

You ask me now, my Darling,
You who wear my only ring,
Why my love for you is deep.

It is the promise you keep:
Christmas nights, two times twelve;
And my sons, times two, as well;

Passion deep, and true friendship;
Pure grace, and companionship;
Full joy, and deep contentment;

Laughter, and true fulfillment.
You are frankincense and myrrh,
And wine for my spirit, Dear.

Oh, my True Love, you must know,
You are the wealth of my soul.

I made an attempt to write a song for My Love's Celebration. A wonderful former student, Ranjeev Cardoza, set it to music and sang it at the Celebration.

The Last Ballad

A long time ago, in a land far away,
lived a young writer, who wrote night and day.
Her gift was so rare, her gift was so great;
but hidden away, oh what a heart break.
Her gift was so rare, from a land far away,
it's far, far away, but so close to home.

A long time ago, in a land far away,
lived a young singer, who sang night and day.
His gift was so rare, his gift was so great;
but hidden away, oh what a heart break.
His gift was so rare, from a land far away,
it's far, far away, but so close to home.

The two artists met, the world rang like a bell;
when true lovers meet, we know it so well.
Oh their love took wing, they made songs so fair;
great songs of power, so sweet and so clear.
This gift was so rare, from a land far away,
it's far, far away, but so close to home.

The young artists' art, was fed by their love.
So how do you gift, a gift from above?
You wrap it in love, and give it in love;
and fortune and fame, will follow your love.
This gift is so rare, from a land far away,
it's far, far away, but so close to home.

They followed their art, so true was their love;
the more that they shared, the more they were loved.
Such a gift so great, writes its own story;
a story of love and, fortune and glory.
This gift is so rare, from a land far away,
it's far, far away, but so close to home.

Their life was so full, their life was so sweet,
their love was great, their blessings complete.
But a candle so bright, burns fast and away.
A lifetime of love, was gone in a day.
This gift is so rare, from a land far away,
it's far, far away, but so close to home.

But a love this great, never fades or dies,
This gift once given, moves beyond the skies.
It moves to that land, that land far away,
a land that's its home, that land far away.
Our lovers yet sing, they sing in that land,
that's far, far away, but now is their home.

Our lovers yet sing, they sing in that land,
that's far, far away, but now is their home.

Ranjeev had demurred, saying we should seek a professional singer for the performance. But, My Love spoke to me and said, no. Ranjeev will sing it with love. And, he did.

I wrote this for My Love on Christmas Day, 1997. As I read it now, I see so well how true the words I wrote that day. Every gift, she gave to me! None could I give her in return!

I Have No Gift for Thee

I have no gift to give you, Love, on this Christmas morn.

I thought and thought and schemed, My Love,
 and strove with all my might.

I thought to give you gold, My Love, but gold I never had, My Love,
 and likely never will.

Then I thought me, Love, to wish for Merlin's powers, Love, that
 magic might I wield.

But gifts divine you have, My Love, beauty, grace and fire, My Love,
 in measures vast.

No art, My Love, no skill could touch such charms, My Love, and
 likely never will.

Then I thought me, Love, to give my heart, my soul, my all, My Love.

But those, My Love, I gave full free to thee when stars were born, and
 light began to shine.

All those you have, My Love, and all that with them go, My Love,
 as you ever will.

I strove, I thought, I schemed, My Love, and yet to no avail.

I thought to give you joy, My Love, and light, and laughter, too.

I cannot give you those, My Love, for those you give to me, My Love,
as you ever will.

Then I thought me, Love, a simple smile, My Love,
how great a smile would be.

Ply, I thought, my skill with words, I thought, and give a smile,
I thought, to thee.

But then, My Love, I thought me, Love, your smiles give gifts to me,
My Love, as they ever will.

Then I knew, My Love, I know, My Love, I have no gift to give.

For light and smiles, tears of joy, love and laughter, too, My Love,
blessings small and great,

Gifts that make the heart to soar, the spirit rise, you give to me,
My Love, as you ever will.

And so I find, My Love, I have no gift to give thee, Love,
on this Christmas morn.

For all the gifts that I might give, My Love, all the gifts, I have,
My Love, first you gave to me.

All the gifts I give thee, Love, you give back to me, My Love,
and I know you ever will.

Oh, how I miss Christmases with My Love. She loved Christmas so!
She loved opening packages, she loved the lights, she loved the snow!
She loved it all, and she loved me the most!

Always spend Christmas with your love, Dear Reader!
Miss not a one!

I penned this for My Love on June 12, 1991. It certainly is not elegant as I read it today, but she liked it so much that she framed it and hung it over her office desk.

Twenty

Twenty years, or is it moons or days, how can I tell?
The glass will tell me straight away, all unkindly.

Far better the reflection of sons, tall, sure and fell.
Bright and strong, they are, and ours so proudly.

Kinder still that which we have wrought rings its bell.
Higher, farther than my wildest dreams, flying boldly.

Our candle burns twain, our voices are a single peal.

We have cast a shadow across the world, so brightly
have our lives flared, mind driven, it seems unreal.

Oh, but how shallow the fame, how callow and flighty,
driven by the green monster, jealousies they unreel.

It matters not, our love surges still, ever sprightly.
Our lives are armored by love, talent, a burning fire.

The fruit of that love, grown, rowing, surging strongly,
every fresh, ever new, always bold, tasting of desire,
lifts, sustain, protects, endears but I say proudly
that its future promise pales the past, quickens the fire.

I know not how long the path that led us her so lightly,
I care only for tomorrow, for tomorrows with you.

I seem to always want to write something for My Love at Christmas time, but my pen seems to fail me utterly on those occasions. Here is something that now embarrasses me, that I wrote in 2001. Weak though it is, it won a smile from My Love and she kissed me so sweetly to reward me for the effort. She could always see through the gift to the heart behind.

Thirty Years of Christmas
My Love Hath Given Me

A band of gold, rare and pure, to have and hold, you gave to me!
  Oh, how precious, this your gift,
    but not the first was this, the gift you gave to me!

A home of love, warm and dear, to bide and rest, you gave to me!
  Oh, how precious, this your gift,
    but not the first was this, the gift you gave to me!

A son of joy, bright and fierce, to love and guard, you gave to me!
  Oh, how precious, this your gift,
    but not the first was this, the gift you gave to me!

Two sons of joy, tall and strong, to watch and love, you gave to me!
  Oh, how precious, this your gift,
    but not the first was this, the gift you gave to me!

A life of love, pure and sweet, to hold and have, you gave to me!
  Oh, how precious, this your gift,
    but not the first was this, the gift you gave to me!

My days of joy, deep and pure, to warm and keep, you gave to me!
  Oh, how precious, these your gifts,
    and now the first was this, your love you gave to me!

We had planned to marry again on our fiftieth wedding anniversary on the beaches of Maui. That was not to be.

I wrote this pledge and I made it solemnly on the day of My Love's Celebration. I think she made her pledge at the same time on the other side of this hateful veil that now separates us!

With this Ring

With this, my ring, I did'st, thee wed, My Love!
Till death, doth part, I did'st, thee wed, but now!
I know, that death, holds not a sting, My Love!
I now, thee wed, 'till time hath run, I vow!

With this, my ring, I do, thee wed, My Love!
Till time doth end, till God doth stop my heart.
I know not how, God doth keep time, My Love.
But plan, He hath, My Love, and death no part!

Our hearts, He bound, I know not how, but did'st.
I wait, My Love, till this, my vow, can'st be.
Our hearts, wert torn, He made them one, He did'st!
I wait, My Love, till I can be, with thee.

With this, my ring, I do thee wed, My Love!
No end, hath time. No end, hath we, My Love!

I do not remember penning this. It is clearly no poem and is so self-centered that it is embarrassing. I clearly wrote it, for it is in my hand, and it was written on June 12, 1979. I found it among My Love's keepsakes. She must have found value in it!

My Wife

To My Wife,
My Friend,
My Lover,
My Life's Companion,
The other half of My Soul,

On this, the eighth anniversary
of our union, I can only say
I love you!
I love the children you have given me!
I love the life you have given me!

My world is complete!

Always!

I wrote this for My Love on June 12, 1983. It is not in verse, but it is a poem that arose from my heart and it still sings to me today.

Sweetheart

You have now given me twelve years of your life. For twelve years, you have loved me and cared for me and kept faith in me. You have given me children—sons whose minds and spirits would make the vainest of men proud. That alone has made me immortal. You have aided me and guided me and shared with me in ways which I sadly fear are foreign, if not unknown, to other couples. You have made my life a constant joy. If I have any accomplishments, they are yours; if I have any achievements, they are yours. I do not understand how other men can live or succeed without the love of such a one as I have had. And yet, I know that such as you are rare. God gives to few the gift that I have. Surely, I am the most blessed of men.

To say that I love you is inadequate—though I say and make you understand that the love is from my heart and my whole self. My one regret is that I have not given as I have received. I have told you but rarely of my love for you. I told you once, when we were but newly wed, that I loved you more with each passing day. I do not believe that I truly understood then, the depth of that simple statement. Though I do not know how such a thing is possible, save as a reflection of your heart, I find it true—and forever a growth of the love between us do I foresee. This life cannot contain such a love. It will burst these mortal bonds.

Often do I ponder the reason that we exist. The power that set the universe in motion, that ordered the laws of the stars, that watched over the development of intelligence is, I think, beyond our ability to comprehend. Ever am I awed by the beauty and grace and intricacy of all of creation. Though I am but a mote on an unremarkable planet, circling an insignificant star, at the outer edge of a small galaxy, wandering about at the periphery of the universe, I do know one truth. It is that love and love alone has the power to explain and to justify the ordering of the universe.

Have I said to you that you have enriched and fulfilled my life? These words evoke but a pale representation of reality. Human communication is but a dark and distorted mirror of the heart and mind. I am told that the ancient Greeks had three words for love in an attempt to explain different planes of the phenomenon. I know not what planes of love may exist, but I do know that my love for you spreads over them all.

My Dearest, please forgive me for being remiss in saying it and being unable to find better words to say it than those which close this epistle.

I love you.

I know that those three words are truly, truly the most powerful words in the universe.

Dear Reader, go say those words to the one you love.
Go say them now!

My Love was always fond of Dream Catchers and the Dream Catcher legend. In 1996, she gave a key note address to an international conference of entrepreneurship scholars in Jyväskylä, Finland. She closed her remarks with this clarion call.

Catching the Dream

Exploring, venturing, striving toward the unseen and the unknown;
envisioning, daring, innovating, changing, seeing what's not there;

Building, ordering, catching the dreams and making them real;
Caring, supporting, encouraging, bringing harmony to the whole;

These are the gifts we possess.
These are the strengths we bring to our cause.

Our nation, our wealth, our common good
are dependent upon these assets—our people.

With common purpose and entrepreneurial goals,
we can, indeed, become the best that we can be.

We must, we can, we will

Catch the Dream

for that is the hope of the future.

I found all of my letters after My Love awakened. She had kept them all in a little box. There were 74 letters, beginning in October, 1965, and continuing until March, 1971, before our wedding in June. The letters made me weep because I had lost all of her letters which matched my scribbles long ago. The early letters paint a picture of a callow youth, filled with hubris. How My Love could handle that, I do not know. She waited for me to grow up, despite the fact that she had suitors throwing rings at her feet.

At last, I became a man.

Here is the last letter in the box. I was 24 years old.

Jo Ann
Saturday, 13 March, 1971
2300 hours

As I put this pen to paper I recall it seems a thousand letters I have written. Letters of all types and intents. Letters telling of infatuation, puppy love, confusion, loneliness, despair, coldness, a hundred other things, all written between the lines. But I've never been able to put my feelings on paper. It seems so cold, this ink, so harsh, this paper. How can I say what is in my heart. I miss you so much tonight, My Darling, I love you, I need you.

Time was, when I would flatter myself by believing I was deft with words, that I could portray any image, project any feeling, simply by applying myself. Now I know better. I've learned enough about life and love to know that I will never be able to put into phrases what I feel for you. You must feel it yourself. I so wish we were together.

You know, it seems I've known and loved you all my life and suddenly I can't picture life without you. I feel so lost, so small, when I'm away from you.

It seems so strange to me, this change in myself. Do you remember the days when I dreamed of being a Soldier of Fortune? I wanted to see and do everything, to learn and live and experience, to be a rolling stone, to taste adventure in life's every breath, to gamble life and fortune and future on each new dawn. I wanted to watch the sands of my life sift through my fingers and see each grain bounce separately, and roll in a different direction. I didn't care whether the world would remember me after those sands were gone, but I wanted it to know I was here.

But, now I'm older, wiser, and changed. I've seen men, boys, die. I've seen children starving, begging. I've heard old men curse the sun for bringing them another day of life and misery. I've seen old women struggling with a load of sticks, their backs bent, their minds blank, emptied by the raging tides of life. I've seen young, beautiful girls sacrifice themselves to the money god. I've seen young men grasping desperately for a moment of happiness, searching for an instant of peace. I, too, have searched for an instant of peace. I, too, have searched for that instant, for so long, and without knowing what it was I searched for.

At last, I know. At last, I see. God, in His infinite wisdom and mercy has blessed me so greatly. Men spend their lives searching for the mysteries of life, searching for a reason to live, a purpose for being. Now that my eyes are open, I can see. The answer is so simple, so close to us all. Can you see it, My Love? You see, only creatures capable of love can live together in this universe, and only those in love can see the reason for living, for being, for creation, is for love.

All God's mysteries and works are revealed in our love. All the world is a stage for us. The universe is our playground. All that is, is for us, so that our love can live and grow, until it carries us to the bosom of our Creator, for in us is He, and only through our love can we see and love Him. At last I've found the answers I sought for so long. I feel so close to complete contentment now. Soon, we'll be together forever. My love is already growing with each passing day. Surely, God will bless us with much happiness. I so wish that the world could know what I know, could feel what I feel, but I know it can't or won't. This earth, and likely this universe, will shortly destroy itself, destroy itself for a lack of feeling, a lack of love. I've seen so few people who love, and so many who hate, even more who don't feel at all. That's the real tragedy of life, not the pain and suffering, for that can be endured through love. But so many die each day without ever having so much as believed in love, without ever knowing a single moment of true peace.

I'm so thankful tonight that we will not be in that number. The world will not remember us, nor even know that we're here, but we won't need or want what it has to give, for we have as our bond, the foundation of everything. What more can we ask.

Another hour has slipped by and it is now Sunday, and I no longer feel alone. I feel very close to you at this moment, and I feel very humble, very blessed. You see, My Love, pride is not a product of love, but humbleness, for as unworthy as I am, God has chosen to give me this most precious gift, and now I no longer fear eternity. Perhaps in that blessed eternity we'll walk hand in hand through the blue black sky and wander about the stars, or weave a garland of sunbeams to light our way through the moon.

Darling, there's so much I want to say, but I can't find the words, and the ones I've written seem so empty and shallow. Read, and reread between these lines of blue, My Love. You must feel what I feel. I can't tell you. I don't know how. I love you more than I can understand myself, and I need you, though I've never needed anyone before. Our lives are about to begin anew. The coming rebirth holds the promise of total contentment, complete happiness. Were it not a sin, I would wish the time away, but it will pass at its own pace, and I trust it will bring us together at last.

Until then, I will send my love on the arms of the moon, the lips of the wind, for this paper is unworthy to carry my heart to you, this pen incapable of speaking my soul.

Darling, I love you.

In April, 2011, our first grandchild, Stella Grace, was born so premature that she could not live. Our daughter in law, the daughter of our hearts, was stricken with preeclampsia and our baby girl was born at only 22 weeks. She lived but an hour, then left this world to return to her home. Forever, will we love her!

Ode to Stella Grace

On wings of love, you swooped and dove, My Darling Dear;
they brushed our lips, they kissed our eyes, and stilled our sighs.

Called you Stella, your Mother did, My Darling Dear;
for stars did shine, from Heaven's Gate, to still our sighs.

A dream you were, sheer gossamer, My Darling Dear;
and tears of love, and tears of joy, did still our sighs.

And called you Grace, your Mother did, My Darling Dear;
and gift you were, so great a gift, you stilled our sighs.

So fierce, so proud, your Mother was, My Darling Dear;
and strong, so strong, your Father was, it stilled our sighs.

So loved you were, so deep and full, My Darling Dear;
as sip you did, of air and love, and stilled our sighs.

So soon you did, unfurl those wings, My Darling Dear;
to fly again, to Heaven's Gate, be still our sighs.

But Mother's Love, and Father's Faith, My Darling Dear;
did give us time, to love you more, and stilled our sighs.

While Angels wait, to fly you home, My Darling Dear;
we drink, we drink, of love so sweet, it stills our sighs.

And now you're gone, on wings of love, My Darling Dear;
bereft we are, without you here, to still our sighs.

But mem'ry serves, and love remains, My Darling Dear;
and strength we draw, from pools of love, to still our sighs.

So small you were, but huge your heart, My Darling Dear;
and loved you were, and loved you are, so still your sighs.

Now time has fled, but love remains, My Darling Dear;
we love you still, we always will, be still our sighs.

On wings of love, you swoop and dive, My Darling Dear;
with Angels fair, in Heaven's air, it stills our sighs.

Our son and daughter came through that tragedy, tempered by fire that no one should have to endure. Stella's little sister now occupies this plane, and beautiful she is, but memory remains and love sustains.

I was so angry. My Love was in so much pain, and nothing would help her. She refused to take the narcotics her physicians prescribed. They numbed her mind as well as her body. She would not tolerate anything that touched her mind. Why, she would say, should I sleep my life away, just to escape the pain? I would rather be awake and with you.

Breast cancer turned to bone cancer, it destroyed my heart. Her courage was so great, but I wept every night that we huddled on our love seat. She could not lie down and I could not leave her. I could only hold her hand and scream at God.

List to Me!

I ask Thee God, please list to me! I pray!
Her pain is great, her spirit strong, so true!
My Love, she needs such care! Your touch she craves!
Please take her pain, I ask Thee God, won't You!

It hurts me so, My Love, to help thee not!
I would'st that I could take thy pain, I cry!
Please, God, give me the pain! I pray it stops!
Give me the pain, Dear God, or tell me why!

We sleep in naps, My Love! I hold thy hand!
The poppy's kiss, dost thou refuse, I know!
I hold thy hand, and kiss that golden band!
To take your pain, My Love, would'st give my soul!

So strong thou art, My Love, and loves thee, me!
So weak I am, My Love, but I love thee!

But always, My Love speaks to me, to turn my mind to the joy we shared. Even in the depths of her pain, she filled me with joy each time she took my hand.

I am certain sure that this little poem, My Love whispered to me. As I was searching photographs I spied a beautiful sunset that we had shot on one of our trips. But, I could not tell from the photograph whether it actually was a sunset or rather, a sunrise.

May the sun always rise for you and your love, Dear Reader.

Sun Rise, Sun Set

Sun rise, sun set, how can'st we know, My Love!
Must wait, must watch, to see, to know, its wend!
Sun set, sun rise, why dost we care, My Dove?
Do we begin, My Love, or do we end?

I know, this quest, My Love, I know, tis clear!
Our love wilt last till time has turn't his glass!
And then, My Love, will not be done, this sphere!
No end, My Love, can'st there e'er be, My Lass!

So this, I know, My Dear, tis clear, sun rise!
No end, My Love, can'st be, My Love, to this!
This is, My Love, e'er clear, My Dear, clear skies!
Our love, My Love, was meant to be, this kiss!

So now, you know, the pict doth show, My Love,
the sun arise, e'er and anon, My Love!

My Love hath bade me close with this, Dear Reader. Thou has read my lines so faithfully, and walked these miles so carefully, I am blest.

I wish for you, so much, Dear Reader! I wish for you a love like mine!
A love that will transcend time!

May that be your blessing, and may you know my joy
without my pain!

This last sonnet is for you. JoAnn whispered it in my ear!

To a Fellow Lover

To list to me so long, My Dear, tis clear!
Thou art in love, wilt be in love, no doubt!
I wish thee love! A love like mine, My Dear!
I hope thou found, a word that to you shouts!

Tis naught but love that led thee here, to me!
A love like mine, a love like thine, so sweet!
Attract, we do, like moths to flames! Me! Thee!
The heat of love is palpable! White heat!

Thee's read my lines, thee's heard me shout, My Friend!
Thee knows my heart! I've laid it bare to thee!
A love so strong, cannot be bound! Nor end!
Hold tight, thy love! Do clasp thy love to thee!

I love thee, Friend, tis clear, for thee art me!
Thee loves me, Friend, I know, for I am thee!

When this came to me, I somehow knew it had to be a sonnet. That's what My Love wanted. And, yet, I thought, how does one build a sonnet around a three syllable word? Sonnets are so highly structured, ten syllables, iambic pentameter, all ordained by the Bard. One deviates from that mold at one's peril! But, as My Love could foresee, I found a way to fold the creatures into the Bard's mold.

This is my final sonnet for thee, Dear Reader. I hope you see the power in these few words, for power there is.

I wish for you, Dear Reader, complete and total joy as you dance and fly with your love on your day!

Butterflies

Butterflies, did I spy today, did'st fly.
Beautiful, did I say, My Love, wert they?
Marvelous, wert the pair, My Love, blue sky!
Fabulous, wert the pair, My Love, did'st play!

Fluttering, kissed my face, such grace, they show!
Palpitant, to mine eye, so sad, so sweet!
Flittering, in the sky, the pair, aglow!
Stupendous, in the race, wert they! Dids't meet!

One day, they live, My Love, one day! Then die!
Their life, their fate, so sad, so sad, so blue!
But love, they have, that day, and so, dost fly!
One day, to love, to live, to fly, so true!

With grace, and love, they dance and fly, they play!
In love, tis theirs, the sky, the world, that day!

I close this tiny tome, Dear Reader, with my most important words. This has been a work of love, and my hope and wish for you is a life of love. You need not be a poet, Dear Reader, to find the words to say to your love. These words, these few words shake my world. I say them still, every day.

Say them to your love, Dear Reader. Say them every day.

I love you, Sweetheart!

Always and forever!

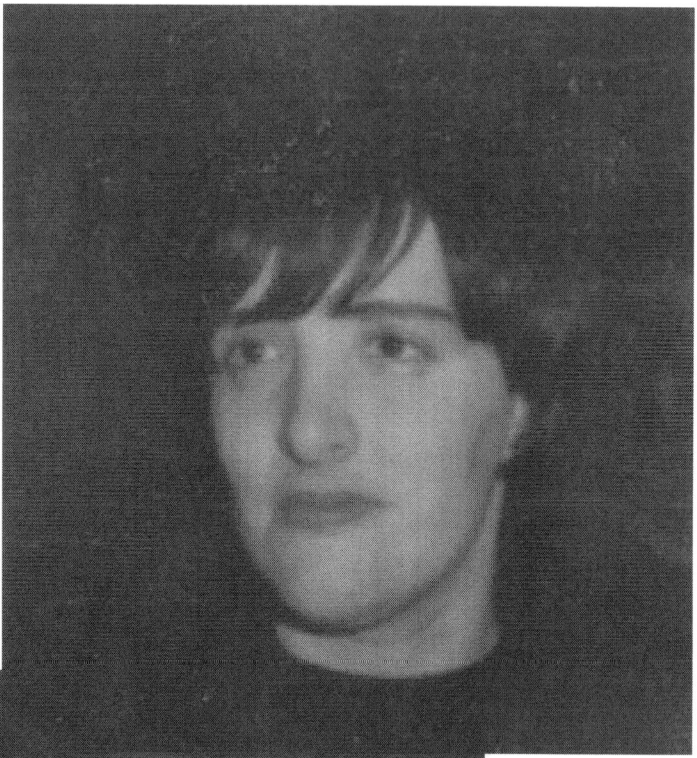

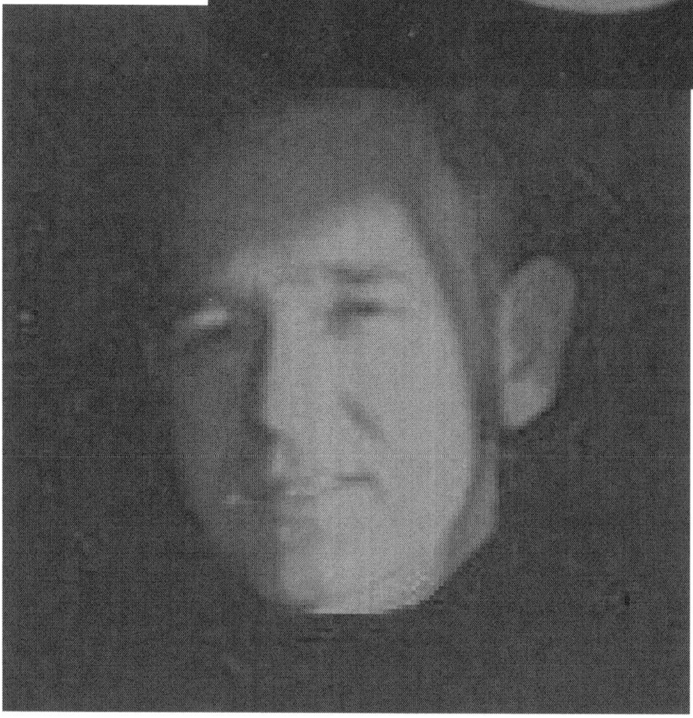